Igor Chigrin

GET FUNDED!

How to Find the Money
to Successfully Grow Your Business
and Solve its Most Pressing Challenges

List of Contributors:
Chapter 14. Scientific Research & Experimental Development (SR&ED) Tax Credit. Lam Tran, Principal Consultant with Advanced Growth Management.
Chapter 15. Customs Duties Drawback and Relief Programs. Win Global Partners, Export & Import Education & Consulting Firm.
Chapter 17. Government Funding for Non-Profit Organizations. Vivian Li, a grant writer specializing in government funding for non-profit organizations and fundraising.
Chapter 18. Angel and Venture Capital Funding. Gerard Buckley, Managing Director of Jaguar Capital and the past Chair of the Board of Maple Leaf Angels.
Chapter 19. Asset-Based Lending & Factoring. Olga Baldin, VP Business Development with Grand Financial Management Inc.
Chapter 20. Equipment Leasing & Financing. Ken Hurwitz, Senior Account Executive with Blue Chip Leasing Corporation.
Chapter 21. Real Estate Financing: Commercial Mortgages. Sam Mahmood, Consultant – Commercial Financial Services with SME Financing.

Printed in Canada

ISBN 978-1-77505-910-3

Fair Grant Writing Limited
+1 (647) 800-5006 | info@fairgrantwriting.ca

To my family for their love and support
To my clients for their trust and business
To my industry peers for their contribution

ABOUT THE AUTHOR

Thank you for reading the book "Get Funded!" This book is based on the author's and contributors' years of experience successfully getting financing for Canadian businesses and non-profit organizations. Its purpose is to help Canadian business owners, senior executives and employees put their thoughts and processes together and submit successful applications for funding, including government grants and loans, bank, private and non-traditional financing.

This book was written by Igor Chigrin, a Business Funding Expert at Fair Grant Writing, a Canadian grant writing company based in the Greater Toronto Area, Ontario, Canada.

Five years ago, Igor was a struggling export consultant with an average of two projects a year. In fact, things were so bad that he had no choice but to take a full-time job to be able to support his growing family. Government funding positively changed his business and transformed it into a thriving practice with an average of six projects a year and a couple of specialty training projects (thanks to leveraging training grants). This whole transformation happened in less than nine months.

Since then, he has become passionate about government financing and committed to positively transforming other businesses by unlocking their access to government funding. This is why this book was written.

Igor Chigrin consults businesses on wide range of Canadian government funding and helps them get non-repayable grants and no interest loans for their growth and expansion.

Igor has a 10-year consulting experience. He holds a Master in International Business degree from Grenoble Graduate School of Business (France) and a Bachelor in Management degree from International University of Business and New Technologies (Russia). He holds the CITP (Certified International Trade Professional) designation.

If, while reading this book, you have any questions or need help with your application for funding, selected documents, or reports, or you just want somebody to look at your application, feel free to reach out to Igor Chigrin and his team at www.FGWinc.ca or contact the author at igor@fgwinc.ca or call +1 (647) 800-5006. We'll be happy to help you out.

CONTENTS

HOW TO DETERMINE YOUR FUNDING NEEDS & SELECT THE RIGHT FUNDING

When it comes to investing in growing your business or organization or solving its most pressing challenges, gaining reliable access to funding is a major concern. According to a Royal Bank of Canada survey, it is the second biggest challenge CFOs face after dealing with government regulations and taxes. So, it is no wonder that as a business or organization leader, executive or employee, you may feel uncomfortable with how you are funding your business or organization.

But what if you need to invest in your business or organization more than once a year, or need a variety of funding options for a project? What if you knew you had reliable access to funding when you needed it, before you needed it? What if you didn't have to rush through the whole application process every time you wanted to expand your business or organization, or invest in a project to address a business challenge?

To make all this happen, you need to start with a proper business plan, which is your first step in determining your funding needs and selecting the right funding.

1. Write a Business Plan

The business plan usually contains several sections, such as management and project team, production, marketing and sales plan, human resources plan, research & development, etc., as applicable. However, for the purposes of this book, we will only focus on business goals, business challenges, capital and operational plans.

If you don't have a business plan yet, make it a priority to write one yourself or hire a third party to help you. All funders will want to see a solid, well thought out business plan for the start-up or growth of your business or organization. Furthermore, you will use the information from the business plan over and over again when applying for funding.

The business plan outlines your business or organization's clear and measurable goals, and the steps you need to take to achieve those goals. **Those steps represent your needs. Anything that prevents you from achieving your goals also represents your needs.** Make a list of what you need to have or do to remove those obstacles.

For example, to achieve your business goal of $10 million in annual sales, you may need 6 employees and an office, or you may need 20 employees, 100,000 square feet of industrial space and 30 pieces of metal forming equipment. Your business or organization's needs may be different from another's, but you can't get funding without first determining them properly.

Once you understand your needs, it is time to categorize and quantify them. There are two categories: capital and operational funding needs. The capital needs are those that occur once and usually include the building, equipment, vehicle and similar needs. The operational needs are those that occur on a regular basis, including wages and salaries, raw materials, fuel, parts, etc. As a result, you must have something like the following example made up for a metal forming shop.

Capital Needs		**Operational Needs (Monthly)**	
Metal Forming Equipment	$250,000	Wages of 2 machine operators	$6,000
Tools	$10,000	Rent	$3,000
Total One-Time	$260,000	**Total Monthly**	$9,000

Now that you have identified and quantified the capital and operational needs, follow this process.

2. Assess Your Resources

Your resources are your own money, or the business or organization's revenues, retained earnings and unpaid dividends. Your assets, and your business or organization's assets and inventory, are also the resources. You can sell unwanted or underutilized assets or part of your inventory. Your resources are your shares, and you can sell them to get funded too. Make a list of resources and quantify them by assigning a dollar value to each resource.

Now ask yourself: Is the dollar value of my resources enough to meet my funding needs? Keep in mind that business revenues are hopefully regular and predictable, so you can rely on them to cover at least your operational expenses. So, if the answer is "Yes," good for your business or organization. It means that your business or organization can self-fund its growth and solve its pressing challenges. If the answer is "No," you need either capital funding to address your capital needs, or operational funding to address your operational needs. Proceed to steps 3 and/or 4, depending on your needs.

3. Address Your Capital Needs

Are you planning to do major one-time investment to start or expand your business or organization? If so, you need capital funding. The funders will need to know your specific intentions for the money to assure themselves that your business or organization will be in a position to repay the funding, if applicable.

The capital funding options include:

- Government Grants
- Government Loans
- Canada Small Business Financing Program
- Angel & Venture Capital Funding
- Equipment Leasing & Financing

- Commercial Real Estate Financing (Commercial Mortgages)
- Crowdfunding (not covered in the book)

4. Address Your Operational (Working Capital) Needs

Are you anticipating or currently having trouble paying your regular obligations on time, including, but not limited to, salaries, rent, materials, parts and utility bills? If so, you need operational funding, also called working capital. The funders will need to know and project your cash flow, i.e. the amount of your regular funding needs (costs) and your regular revenue, to assure that your business or organization will be in a position to repay the funding, if applicable.

The operational funding options include:

- Scientific Research & Experimental Development Tax Credit (SR&ED) and other Tax Credits (e.g. Apprenticeship Training Tax Credit, Interactive Digital Media Tax Credit, etc. – not covered in the book)
- Customs Duty Drawback
- Asset-Based Lending & Factoring
- Credit Cards (not covered in the book)
- Lines of Credit (not covered in the book)
- Term Loans (not covered in the book)

5. Research the Options

Once you've selected the right funding options for your business or organization, research them further. Find 2-3 funders for each option. If you have trouble finding the funders, ask your accountant, banker, employees or industry peers. Contact each funder to discuss your funding needs to get a sense of the terms of funding and to gauge their relevance to your business or organization's goals before you apply.

6. Apply Early

It is always better to anticipate your funding needs rather than look for money under pressure when you are about to do what you've planned. It is harder to get approval for funding when your business or organization is already in trouble, so plan ahead and secure funding well in advance to meet application deadlines that may be in place. Sometimes it takes months to get approved. Use the information from your business plan to apply for funding. Make sure that you have a written record of the funding approval before you start spending money. This way, you'll be able to get the funding far sooner than a regular reactive approach would allow.

SECTION 1.

GOVERNMENT FUNDING

In this section, we're going to provide Canadian business owners and managers with valuable tips on how to write a compelling grant proposal, and practical, step-by-step guidance on how to manage the grant writing process. While working on this book, we tried to put the information together and present it in an easy-to-understand way, enriched by tips and recommendations. Although its content is adapted to fit the interests of private-sector enterprises, non-profit organizations may also find it applicable to their cases.

In this section, we will also demystify government grants and respond to the common questions and concerns that we've heard over the years from our clients in manufacturing, research & development, professional services and non-profit sectors. We hope this book will help you to prepare winning applications for government grants and loans, and that you receive the money to solve your most pressing business challenges.

Let's get started.

CHAPTER 1.

WHAT IS GOVERNMENT FUNDING?

Government funding is the type of financing where the government or its authorized agents contribute money directly to for-profit businesses or non-profit organizations, research and educational institutions, and other legal entities.

There are three major forms of funding for businesses provided by all levels of the Government of Canada and the municipalities:

- A **Government Grant** is non-repayable funding awarded to the for-profit business for certain purposes; for example, purchasing equipment, expansion, skills training, hiring, export marketing, etc. The application for the government grant must be submitted and approved before the start of the project.

- A **Government Loan** is repayable funding typically for large-scale expansion, research & development, and commercialization projects. The conditions of the government loans typically include a 0%- or low-interest rate, a grace period of up to 12 months following project completion, no collateral, and no ownership of the intellectual property resulting from the project being financed by the government. The application for the government loan must be submitted, and in most cases approved, before the start of the project.

- A **Tax Credit** is non-repayable funding awarded retroactively to the for-profit business for certain purposes; for example, research & development, hiring, or training projects. The application for the tax credit must be submitted along with the corporate tax return.

Major advantages of government funding include either non-repayment when taking out the government grant or the tax credit, and a zero- or low-interest rate when taking out the government loan.

Going forward, you'll find many special terms used during the funding application process. Let us explain these terms in the next section (Glossary).

CHAPTER 2.

GLOSSARY

Here are some frequently used words that you may come across while studying government funding guidelines and preparing your application package.

Application – the set of forms, supportive documents and calculation sheets, if applicable, that must be submitted to the funder to apply for the government grant or loan.

Applicant – the legal entity applying for the government grant or loan.

Contribution – the amount of the government grant or loan allocated to the approved applicant.

Contribution Agreement – the legally binding document signed by the approved applicant and the government or its authorized agents that contains the terms and conditions of the contribution, project timelines, goals, and other terms.

Disbursement – the process of transferring money from the government or its authorized agents to the approved applicant's bank account.

Eligibility – the set of mandatory rules and criteria that must be met by the applicant and the applicant's project to be able to apply for the government grant or loan.

Government Grant – non-repayable contribution from the government or its authorized agents.

Government Loan – repayable contribution from the government or its authorized agents.

In-Kind Contribution – non-monetary contribution (free services, donated materials, labour equipment, or space). The market value of such contributions must be secured in the form of a letter from the supplier.

Intake Period – the limited period when the applicants can apply for the government grant or loan. Failure to respect the intake period will result in immediate rejection of the application.

Leverage – the share of a funder's contribution to the total project budget.

Stacking Limit – the limit of government funding that may be allocated for the same project or cost by other government funders.

Matching Funds – the amount of money that the approved applicant must secure on top of government funding to complete the approved project.

Submission – the process of transmitting the application to the government or its authorized agents.

Now that you know the terminology, it's time to find out the steps you'll follow during the grant writing process.

CHAPTER 3.

THE 10 PHASES
OF A GRANT WRITING PROJECT

Typically, the grant writing project consists of the following phases, and you will find more about each phase below:

1. Defining the project(s) to be funded
2. Selecting the government grant or loan program
3. Researching the selected government grant or loan program
4. Gathering information
5. Gathering supportive documentation
6. Budgeting for the project
7. Writing, reviewing, and proofreading the proposal or application
8. Submitting the application and incorporating feedback
9. Executing the funded project
10. Writing the report or claim

Key project milestones are things such as making the decision to apply or not to apply for a grant or loan, completing the application, receiving a funding decision by the government funding agency, and receiving the contributions.

Key deliverables are things such as the application itself and the government funding being deposited into your bank account.

Defining the project(s) to be funded. The government does not grant money just because your business meets eligibility criteria. The money is only available for use on specific business-led projects like product development or productivity improvement, skills training, export marketing, etc. The project must have clear goals, deliverables, and measurable benefits. The project must have human, financial, and other resources assigned. The project must have start and end dates and milestones. The roles and responsibilities in the project must be clearly separated and well-defined.

Selecting the government grant or loan program. Study all government grant and loan programs applicable to your project; for example, all grants for research & development. Study their goals, funding priorities, eligibility criteria, and a list of eligible and ineligible costs carefully. Match this information to your project's scope and expected outcomes and decide whether it meets the word and the spirit of the government programs you selected. Then, choose the most fitting program. It is better to find a grant program to fit your project, rather than try to create a project to match a government grant or loan program.

Researching the selected government grant or loan program. Further study the selected program, including its application forms, application timelines, process, and evaluation criteria. Scope out the grant writing project: define goals and deliverables, set the timeline, and assign resources. As mentioned, grant writing takes time, so don't leave the application until the last minute. Ideally, apply two to three months before the submission deadline and plan your grant writing activities accordingly. Work with your favourite project management and calendar tools to keep track of the grant writing.

Gathering information. You will most likely need input from sources both inside and outside your organization to complete the proposal or application. You may need information from your engineers, accountants, customers, or service providers, so allocate enough time to secure the feedback from these parties.

Gathering supportive documentation. Like information gathering, this phase typically involves gathering quotes, estimates, or proposals from third parties, as well as internal documentation, such as business plans, financial statements, and sales forecasts.

Budgeting for the project. Typically, each government program has a template for the budget. Follow it carefully. If it is not available, use a common-sense approach and group the costs by capital, operational, management (administration) cost, and in-kind (volunteer) contributions, if the latter is applicable.

Writing, reviewing, and proofreading the proposal or application. Once the information has been collected, put the proposal or application draft together. Just write. Don't worry too much about grammar or spelling at this time – you can correct it later before the submission. Use the templates and forms provided by the funder's (or funders') or online application portal, if available.

Don't exceed the word or character limit if specified by the funder. Once the draft is complete, go through it yourself, then share it with your team, your colleagues, business owners, or anyone else who can make a positive impact and provide feedback on the application. Brainstorm with others on the questions in the application. Incorporate team feedback and ideas right away if they make sense. Then, proofread and make sure that all questions have been answered, and attach supportive documentation if required. Ensure that you have all references, cites, tables, graphs, and pictures in place if they are required.

Have someone who is unfamiliar with the project read the application and tell you whether it makes sense or not. Read the final version of the application aloud if it helps you catch any missing information. Use the application checklist (if provided by the funder) to make sure that you submit the complete application. Sign and date the application. Save a copy of the application and all supportive documentation in case they get lost on the way to the funder.

Submitting the application and incorporating feedback. Submit the application the way the funder has specified: by email, via online application forms, by mail, in person, etc. Seek receipt acknowledgment for the application from the funder. If submitted early enough, you have a chance to get good quality feedback from the grant or loan program administrators. They will advise if there's anything you need to do to strengthen or improve your proposal. Respond to their feedback right away if they have indicated that they have time to talk to you.

Executing the funded project. By this phase, you should receive the approval of your application, and in some cases, even a lump sum of government money upfront. It is now time to deliver what was promised. Failure to do so may result in the government's money-back request. If the circumstances change and you can no longer achieve your goals, you must immediately inform the program administration and seek resolution of the situation together.

Writing the report or claim. Keep track of all project activities, achievements, and costs in a separate folder. Keep proof of payments, such as cancelled (stamped) cheques, bank statements, or money-transfer slips. All government grant and loan programs require a final report at the end of the project, while the number of intermediary reports or claims may vary from one-time to monthly submissions.

So, the first two steps in the grant writing process are 1) choosing a funding program, and 2) selecting a project. Let's talk about them in the next chapter.

CHAPTER 4.

HOW TO FIND AND SELECT THE RIGHT GOVERNMENT GRANTS & LOANS FOR YOUR BUSINESS PROJECTS

Let's start with funding programs selection, and then we'll discuss how to choose the correct projects. You can also start vice versa — both ways work.

There are many different government grant and loan programs available to for-profit businesses. About 70% of all government grants and loans are available for manufacturers or commercial enterprises conducting research & development on a regular basis. Exportable service industries, such as research & development, consulting, engineering, architecture, construction, and design, may be eligible for specific grant programs.

Grants and loans for businesses are typically provincial, regional (for example, funding programs for Atlantic Canada or Western Canada), national (federal), and international (for joint projects with certain countries). There are grants and government loans that are available to specific industries, such as clean tech, automotive, aerospace, etc.

Grants for businesses usually support activities resulting in job growth, skills or capacity improvement, productivity or quality improvement, equipment upgrades, export business development, research & development, and the commercialization of new products. Each program supports only one (maximum two) type of activity. Government loans for businesses usually support large-scale research & development or expansion activities.

So, what is the best way to find the grant program that meets your needs?

First, talk to your industry association representative. If you don't succeed, speak to a representative of your local economic development group, or the ministry of economic/business development. Ask them whether there is any government grant program that fits your business goals.

If you prefer to do the research yourself, here are few suggested websites:

1. Canada Business
   www.canadabusiness.ca/grants-and-financing/government-grants-and-financing
2. National Research Council's Concierge Service
   https://concierge.innovation.gc.ca/en/find-funding
3. Industry Canada's Catalogue of Government Programs
   http://www.ic.gc.ca/eic/site/054.nsf/eng/home
4. Fair Grant Writing Website www.fairgrantwriting.ca, where you can browse the available grant programs grouped by province, purpose and industry and request your free digital catalogue of Canadian government grants and loans for businesses.

Now, select the right project to fund. Most likely, you have multiple projects going on in your organization, such as equipment upgrades, software implementation, productivity improvement initiatives, etc. To select the right project for government funding:

1. Write down a list of upcoming project ideas on a piece of paper or whiteboard.
2. Prioritize the projects by their importance for your organization.

3. Select the projects that have been well-defined (activities, deliverables, and budgets are known).
4. Select the projects that have resources committed to them (human, material, financial, etc.).
5. Select the projects that have stakeholders, employees, or community support.
6. Select the projects that have a greater impact on the business, industry, and community.
7. Select the projects for which the government funding programs have been identified.

Once you find and select funding programs for your business and select the right project, you can move on to the grant writing process.

CHAPTER 5.

TOP 10 ITEMS REQUIRED ON MOST APPLICATION FORMS

Now, grant writing becomes a separate project, so you should define it, prioritize it, and allocate resources toward it. Allocate between 50 and 240 business hours toward the grant writing project. Yes, it does take time to prepare successful applications, especially for those who don't do it on a regular basis.

Each government grant or loan program has different application forms, templates, and evaluation criteria. However, there are some similarities between them. For example, every program requests your contact information. Here are the other items that are common in government grant or loan application forms for businesses.

1. Describe your company, products, or services.
2. Describe your mission, unique value proposition, and competitive advantage.
3. Describe your proposed project: its goals, outcomes, and timelines.
4. Describe the benefits of your project.
5. Explain why this project is important to you.
6. Provide evidence that your company can successfully execute the proposed project.
7. Indicate who within and without your company will be involved in the proposed project and what their roles will be.
8. Outline the proposed project's cost (budget), and provide evidence that you can finance the portion of the proposed project that won't be financed by the funding agency.
9. Outline the proposed project's risks and mitigation strategies.

10. Explain how you will manage the project and track its outcomes.

There are, of course, many additional questions that must be answered in each case. If you are not sure how to answer the question, contact the funder or look for clarification in the application guidelines.

Before diving into writing your application, we suggest you learn what will help you prepare a winning application and save you time.

CHAPTER 6.

CRITICAL SUCCESS FACTORS FOR WRITING A WINNING GRANT APPLICATION

First, there are some recommendations that you should follow to prepare a winning application from an organization/management perspective.

1. **Manage grant writing as a project**. Get organized. File all documents (letters of intent, quotes, estimates, plans, etc.) in a separate folder for each program you apply for. Track the status and amounts of each grant or loan application. Manage tasks for yourself and your team to achieve milestones (application, meetings, suppliers' quotes, government responses, funding, etc.). Make sure that you submit the application before the deadline. Report any changes to the project or your contact information to the funder immediately if they happen after the submission.

2. **Build relationships with funding agencies.** Study funders' websites, and download and read application forms, templates, and guidelines. Based on that research, identify the goals and priorities of the funders and address these in your project and application. Ensure that you know the submission deadlines, eligibility requirements and eligible cost, proposal format, submission instructions, evaluation process and timeline, award criteria, and the maximum amount of funding.

   Find the name, phone number, and email of the contact person (funding officer or manager), and give them a call to introduce yourself, your project, and your organization. Reconfirm the funders' mandate, average funding request amounts, your organization's eligibility, eligible activities, the application format, the application process, time frame, intake deadlines, awarded and rejected past projects, and opportunities for coaching by the funder.

Be open to work with the funder, share the draft application with them, and incorporate their feedback. If possible, attend a funder's introductory seminar or webinar on the government grant or loan program you've chosen. Apply early, seek the funders' feedback, and incorporate it.

3. **Exercise leadership skills**. Government grants and loans typically have strict timelines, so it is important to organize different people or departments to manage information collection and the entire writing process. You can do this by engaging with your employees, partners, or co-workers and expressing your enthusiasm about the initiative you are seeking funding for. In some cases, even formal teams may be created.

Once you are organized, make sure to use the following **12 tips to write a winning grant application**:

1. Follow the program's templates, forms, proposal requirements, and instructions carefully. Be consistent and straightforward.

2. Select a unique project name. Keep it clear and concise. Include outcomes in the name of your project. How does your application stand out?

3. Highlight economic, social, environmental, and other benefits right away. Relate the benefits to the outcomes of your projects. Highlight the return on investment for funders, if it is possible to calculate it. Highlight the long-

term legacy of the project.

4. Use a positive approach in the project description. Outline the scope clearly and concisely, and make sure you write for a non-expert audience. Outline how the project's scope will be addressed and how the outcomes will be achieved.

5. Describe your motivation and project rationale. Let the funder know why you need this project and why the funder should be interested and involved. What is in it for the funder?

6. Demonstrate your company's capacity and capability to execute the project. Describe the company mission and mandate, its unique value proposition, and its competitive advantage. Highlight key employees' or owners' expertise, skills, and abilities to sustain the outcomes. Support your goals with the numbers; for example, results of market or customer research, letters of intent, etc.

7. Demonstrate project partnership. Include community support and roles of partners or suppliers in the project (their areas of responsibility and expertise).

8. Include project timelines. Identify key dates for required financing, project start and completion, and milestones.

9. Assess project risks. Clearly identify the risks and mitigation strategies. What can go wrong with the project and deliverables, and how are you going to address this? Respond to all possible objections by the funder.

10. Clearly indicate the budget, with separate capital, operational, management (administration) cost, and in-kind (volunteer) contribution. The budget must be reasonable and meet the program requirements and expectations.

11. Demonstrate confirmed funding or your ability to acquire it within a reasonable time and at a reasonable cost. Attach contributors' letters of commitment, term sheets, or other proof. Specify if there is any donated money or other resources.

12. Follow the process: Create a draft of the proposal -> Review it in your organization -> Incorporate the feedback -> Make final project outline revisions -> Submit

In the next chapter, you'll find examples of good and bad answers to common application questions. Keep an open mind and try to use those recommendations for your own case.

CHAPTER 7.

EXAMPLES OF GOOD AND BAD ANSWERS TO GRANT APPLICATION QUESTIONS

Below are examples of how you should and should not answer typical questions in government grant application forms or proposal requirements. As an example, let's use the case of furniture manufacturer ABC applying for a grant to increase its productivity by purchasing a CNC woodworking machine.

Question 1. Describe your company, its products (services), and history

Bad Answer

We are a medium-sized manufacturer of home and office furniture in the Toronto area and have been in business for two generations. Our products are sold by major retailers and distributors.

Good Answer

ABC Furniture Manufacturing has been serving customers in the Greater Toronto Area for more than 40 years. The company was founded by Mr. John Smith, a furniture craftsman who was taught by European designers and brought outstanding quality to Canadian furniture design. Mr. Smith quickly expanded the company and educated a core group of designers, who have been following his values since. Mr. Joe Smith, a son of the founder, is now leading the company and has an ambitious agenda to grow the business outside local boundaries.

ABC Furniture Manufacturing has two product lines – office furniture (office chairs, bar chairs, cafeteria chairs, and recreational chairs) and home furniture (sofas and armchairs). The products are sold by major retailers, such as Martin's, Doe's, and Door-Mart. Office furniture is distributed by United Distributor and can be found in the First Country Bank, National Museum, and Observatory. All products are designed by Top-10 national designers and can be customized to meet customers' requirements.

ABC Furniture Manufacturing manufactures products worth $10,000,000 annually.

ABC Furniture Manufacturing is a privately-owned corporation employing 31 full-time employees and between three and five seasonal workers during the high season. Every employee shares our mission and goes through regular training.

ABC Furniture Manufacturing runs a continuous improvement initiative and is ISO (The International Organization for Standardization) certified.

Question 2. Describe your project: its goals and benefits

Bad Answer

We want to buy a new CNC machine to be able to produce the frames for the furniture faster and cheaper.

Good Answer

The goal of the project is to increase frame manufacturing productivity by 20%.

ABC Furniture Manufacturing will achieve this goal through the purchase, installation, and commission of the XYZ Horizontal CNC Machining Center, Model 1500-CWX. This model is the only one available in the market that can meet our needs.

The project phases are as follows:

- Purchasing the CNC Machining Center

- Delivery

- Installation

- Mandatory Training of Machine Operators

- Installing Machine Software

- Tooling

- Tuning and Commissioning

XYZ Horizontal CNC Machining Center, Model 1500-CWX will be fully operational by November 2014.

The benefits are:

- One full-time operator will be hired

- Manufacturing time will drop on average by 20% per part, which will result in an average savings of $4.36 per part

- Precision will be increased to 99% (as compared to 85% today)

- Production capacity will increase by 20%, which will result in additional business opportunities from $2,000,000 of taxable revenue

- Local Institute of Technology will be engaged to conduct operator training ($7,500 in training costs).

Question 3. Why is the project important?

Bad Answer

We need the project because this is a very competitive market and we maxed our capacity.

Good Answer

ABC Furniture Manufacturing is in a price-driven, competitive market. In order to stay in business and continue to grow, we need to constantly improve our processes and find ways to reduce costs. Furniture manufacturing is one of the most resource-, labour-, and capital-intensive businesses.

A few findings triggered this project:

1. Our existing equipment is 100% loaded, and we have no capacity to accept new orders. This situation creates a backlog. On average, delays cost us $375 per order in penalties and shipping costs.

2. Our products are, on average, 10% more expensive than the identical products of our competitor.

3. As a result, our closing ratio dropped from 37% to 29% compared to our last fiscal year.

The current situation is unacceptable, and it threatens the long-term prosperity of our company and its 31 employees, several suppliers, and contractors. The situation doesn't allow us to accept new orders that could result in growing our taxable revenue.

Question 4. How can your company ensure that it will deliver the proposed project?

Bad Answer

We employ folks that know what they are doing and are pretty sure they can get that machine up and running pretty quickly.

Good Answer

The project team will consist of the owner, the chief operations officer (COO), and several subcontracted service providers.

Our COO, Douglas Doe, has been working in furniture manufacturing for the last 23 years. He is a member of the Local Society of Engineers and holds furniture industry distinctions. His experience and knowledge includes furniture design, manufacturing, process optimization, and quality assurance.

Mr. Doe monitors our capacity, and raised a red flag when we reached it. He conducted the research on the equipment that can solve the problem and considered quotes from five different vendors before he selected the one we are purchasing.

Douglas will oversee purchasing, installation, tooling, and other phases of the project, and will work with the following subcontractors:

- Goodman Machinery has been in the business of equipment moving, wiring, and installation for the last seven years.
- Youngman Tooling will provide us with the tools for the new equipment, just as they have been doing for the last 12 years.

The COO and the owner will be responsible for recruiting the machine operator, who will be trained at the Local Institute of Technology, an accredited national certification agency for CNC machine operation training. There will be a minimum of 96 hours of training before the operator starts working.

ABC Furniture Manufacturing allocated $100,000 for the project from our continuous improvement budget. Additionally, between $20,000 and $30,000 may be taken out as an equipment loan or line of credit at the First Country Bank.

Question 5. What is your project's timeline?

Bad Answer

If we buy it tomorrow, it will take us between three and five months.

Good Answer

The estimated project start date is August 1, 2022.

The estimated project end date is November 30, 2022.

More precisely, here is the timeline of the project phases:

- Purchasing CNC Machining Center: August 1 - 31, 2022

- Delivery: September 1 - 14, 2022

- Installation: September 15 - 30, 2022

- Mandatory Training of Machine Operators: October 1 - November 30, 2022

- Installing Machine Software: October 1 - 10, 2022

- Tooling: October 1 - November 20, 2022

- Tuning and Commissioning: November 21 - 30, 2022

Your application is now complete. Follow the funder's instructions to submit the application. Some funders have dedicated online application portals. Others accept applications by email or regular mail. Read the submission instructions carefully. What should you expect next? Find out in the next chapter.

CHAPTER 8.

NEXT STEPS AFTER THE GOVERNMENT GRANT APPLICATION IS SUBMITTED

Take the following steps after your application is submitted. The order doesn't matter. What matters is you complete them all as soon as possible after the submission.

- Make sure that the funder received your application. Expect an email, letter, or phone call. If you haven't heard anything back in five business days, call the funder to ensure the application has been delivered.

- Keep a copy of the confirmation email, receipt from the post office, or other proof on file.

- Have a copy of the application handy to provide fast responses to the government grant or loan program if they ask any questions.

- Highlight the dates you expect to hear back on the application in your calendar. On average, it takes the funder 4 to 24 weeks to assess the application. Typically, the application guidelines will give you application assessment timelines. Contact the funder if you don't hear anything from them within those timelines.

Fortunately, your to-do list in this chapter is not too long. You've already done lots of work. Let's open the curtain and learn how your application is assessed.

CHAPTER 9.

HOW GOVERNMENT GRANT APPLICATIONS ARE ASSESSED

Each grant program employs the help of a group of 3 to 10 industry professionals that review and assess the applications. This group may be called a "proposal review committee," "funding review committee," "grant review committee," "jury," "expert panel," etc. The group's role is to study the proposals, assess them according to the assessment guidelines, and provide funding recommendations.

When you submit your application, it first goes through a consistency check. A junior clerk verifies that:

- All required questions are answered

- All required documents are attached

- The application is signed (if applicable) and dated correctly

- The application is submitted before the deadline

At this time, the application may be rejected, regardless of the value or benefits of your project, if it fails to check all the above requirements.

If the application is consistent, it goes to reviewers. A reviewer may assess the entire application or its parts, depending on the assessment guideline. The assessment guideline typically outlines the requirements of the project and the answers in the application package that a reviewer grades by a certain scale. A reviewer will only be able to assess the application based on what is actually written in it. If it is missing something, there is no way a reviewer will be able to know, guess, or assume.

Typically, reviewers assess the following:

- Depth of short- and long-term positive economic, social, community, or environmental impact of the project (return on the government's investment)

- Company's track record of growth, innovation, and profitability

- Project goals, scope, risks, timeline, and achievability

- Expertise, capacity, and capability of the project team to execute the project

- Stakeholder, partner, and community support for the project

- Financial commitment to the project, and funding sources other than government financing

- Support of evidence, forecasts, and assumptions

Then, the reviewers get together to evaluate all applications at the same time and provide the recommendation for funding. This is when the funding decisions are typically made. The result of the meeting will be a recommendation to approve entirely, approve partially, or decline the application. Note that the funder maintains the minutes of the review meetings and all records in writing so that you can request a debriefing if you disagree with the decision.

After the positive funding recommendations are provided, the applications go to the funder's senior officials for a sign-off. Once they approve, the funder notifies the applicant and issues a contribution agreement. A contribution agreement is the agreement that you sign with the government that obligates you to execute your project within a specific time frame and achieve specific goals in exchange for government financing.

Yes! Your application is approved! What's next?

CHAPTER 10.

NEXT STEPS AFTER GOVERNMENT GRANT APPLICATION IS APPROVED

First, you will receive written notification of your approval, along with the contribution agreement, by email or regular mail. Read the agreement thoroughly, as it contains requirements for your project that must be met. It also contains the schedule of the government contribution (or the conditions upon which you receive the contribution) and the amount of each contribution. Get in touch with the funder immediately if you notice any discrepancy in the agreement or want to negotiate it. Sometimes, the funder approves only some of the costs, but you still have a chance to try to convince the funder to cover other costs, as well.

Run the contribution agreement by your board of directors, advisors, or lawyers if it is customary in your company. The contribution agreement must be signed by the senior executive of the company who has signing authority. Once the document is signed, send a copy back to the funder.

It is now time to deliver your project. Keep track of your time, expenses, and outcomes. Establish a tracking or data collection system from the start. Keep time logs, invoices, receipts, proof of payments, protocols, measurement results, etc. in a separate folder in print and electronic formats. All of this will be extremely helpful and save you time when it is required to report to the government.

Each grant program has different reporting requirements. All of them require a final report and either monthly or quarterly intermediary reports or claims. Reporting requirements can be found in the contribution agreement or funder's guidelines and typically ask you to provide the following information:

1. Actual project timeline versus planned
2. Actual project cost versus planned
3. Project status update (activity report)
4. Project performance update (to what extent the project goals have been achieved)
5. Explanation of any differences, changes, delays, overachievements, etc.

Immediately contact the funder if there are any changes or issues that affect the funded project. Don't wait until you need to report it; by that time, it may be too late. Remember, if you don't deliver the project, not only can the government cancel the next contribution, it may also request a full refund of the previous contributions.

Be accurate, honest, and timely with reporting. Reports are often prerequisites for the contributions. Keep a copy of every report in case it gets lost or you are audited by the funder.

But, what if your application is declined? Let's talk about that scenario in the next chapter.

CHAPTER 11.

10 MOST COMMON REASONS WHY GOVERNMENT GRANT OR LOAN APPLICATIONS ARE DECLINED AND HOW TO AVOID THE REJECTION

1. **Applicant's company or project does not meet eligibility criteria or application timeline**. Read eligibility criteria carefully and make sure that you will qualify. Keep in mind that there are three types of eligibility: eligibility of the company, eligibility of the project, and eligibility of the cost. If you are uncertain about your eligibility, go to www.FGWinc.ca/contact, fill in the form to set up an appointment, and we'll help you check it.

2. **The application is incomplete**. When mandatory fields are left blank or requested attachments or appendices are missing, the application fails the consistency check and is immediately declined. Refer to the appendices if necessary, but provide the references to the appendices in the respective sections or fields of the application. Don't just write "See attachment." As a matter of courtesy, do not attach anything that isn't required for the application. Don't leave any fields blank. If the question is not applicable to your project, write the answer "Not Applicable."

3. **Failure to provide requested additional information**. The government grant or loan program officials may request additional information to support the application before and during application writing, or after the application is submitted. This information may include your company's or employees' background, proposed project information, documents from your customers and suppliers, financials, invoices or quotes, etc. Make sure to provide them as soon as possible.

4. **The application is misleading, confusing, or unrealistic**. Avoid generalizations, logical flaws, data and fact discrepancies, unrequired information, missing information, flood, unsupported budget, forecast and other numbers, and industry acronyms or jargon. Keep in mind that the person who reads and assesses the application does not necessarily possess your knowledge of the industry, technology, service, or product. Try to imagine a 10-year-old child reading your application and write it so that she will understand.

5. **Applicant's financials are not in good shape**. It is too risky for the government to invest in businesses that do not have a track record of profitability and growth. Look at your recent financial statements. If you notice a lack of or sharp decline in sales and inventory, or if there is debt growth, declining profits, and growing losses, then it is probably too early or too late to apply for the government grant. You may apply as soon as the situation gets better.

6. **Failure to demonstrate benefits to the government**. From the government's perspective, the purpose of grant funding is not only to ensure the applicant's long-term growth and prosperity, but also to create value for the public and community. This value must be explicit, measurable, and compelling, and typically includes:
   - Local employment growth in number of jobs created and retained

- Taxable revenue and profit growth in dollar value
- Export sales growth in dollar value
- Community involvement growth in terms of the number of community initiatives and a dollar value
- Spillover effect, meaning engaging businesses and institutions inside and outside of your local area (for example, universities or colleges, suppliers, subcontractors) in terms of the number of impacted entities and a dollar value.

7. **Lack of resources to perform the project**. This reason is not limited to financial resources. Obviously, you should already have or be able to obtain financing to match the government contribution. However, it is also important for you to have sufficient human resources and the technical skills and capabilities to perform the project. In some cases, access to sufficient energy or material sources is critical. The government will also look for proof that you already possess those resources or are able to acquire them.

8. **Competition**. It is very common for several grant applications to be submitted within the same time frame that are competing for a limited amount of funding. As a result, the grant administrators must decide to approve or decline applications, even if they are legitimate and eligible. In this case, the funder will consider your application in comparison to the others, and will approve those that promise a greater benefit to the public or look unique and more realistic.

9. **The government runs out of funding**. The budgets of grant programs are limited; therefore, it is important to apply as early as possible. Don't give up if the funding program you wanted to apply for is out of money. Ask the program management if and when the renewal is expected and mark that date in your calendar. You can resubmit the

application as soon as more funding is available.

10. **The applicant missed the submission deadline**. Many grant programs have limited intake periods that typically last from one to three months. Missing those deadlines makes your project automatically ineligible. Don't delay finding out the deadlines of government funding programs.

Chapter 12.

WHAT TO DO IF A GOVERNMENT GRANT OR LOAN APPLICATION IS DECLINED

A government grant rejection is one of the most discouraging and disappointing events you will deal with in your business, especially considering all the time and effort it took to prepare the application package. First and foremost, calm down and give yourself a day or two to process the decision. Try not to think about the rejection. Remember, the rejection does not mean that your idea, business, application package, or project is bad. It is not the right time to give up. Don't go to war with the funder; instead, try to keep positive business relationships.

First and foremost, ask the funder the reason for the decline. In many cases, the reason is a lack of funding. The funder may have run out of money, since every government grant or loan program has a limited budget. Or, perhaps there were too many applications competing for the grant. Ask the funder when you can resubmit your application. In other words, try to determine when the funder expects to receive more money from the government.

If the reason for the decline is in the application, request a debriefing. By law, funders must maintain written records of the assessment and the decision-making processes and release them to the applicants upon request. Upon receipt of the feedback, go through it on your own (or with your team), then contact the funder if you think the reasons for declining funding were incorrect based on the assessment guideline or if the reviewers may have missed something in the application package. If the reason for the decline looks appropriate, ask how your application can be improved next time and if it can be resubmitted later. Sometimes you can resubmit your application the next month or quarter.

Alternatively, ask the funder if they are aware of any other government grant or loan programs that may contribute to your project.

Generally speaking, receiving a rejection from a funding agency is not good. Let's draw your attention to ways you can increase your chances of success.

Chapter 13.

HOW TO INCREASE YOUR CHANCES OF SUCCESSFULLY APPLYING FOR A GOVERNMENT GRANT OR LOAN

As you've probably realized by now, government grants and loans are one of the most inexpensive (not to say "free") sources of funding for productivity improvement initiatives, equipment purchase or upgrades, export business development, skills training, research & development, and other projects. Yes, the application process can be complex and challenging, but the benefits are great.

After you've decided that government grant or loan funding is right for your business, you have three options:

1. Write your grant or loan application yourself
2. Have your employees write a grant or loan application for your business
3. Use a professional grant writing company that specializes in preparing government funding applications and reports for businesses, such as Fair Grant Writing

If you choose options 1 or 2, we highly recommend that you or your employees read this book again, and estimate the time that is required to find the grant, define the project, write the application package and all reports, and communicate with government representatives.

A tip for you: It takes a professional business grant writer between 50 and 240 business hours to complete an application, depending on the program. Now, multiply those numbers by your or your employee's hourly rate, then add the cost of missed opportunities from dedicating the time to this project. Add supplies and materials. Now, ask yourself, "Is it better to spend that much time and money, or should I hire a professional grant writing company that specializes in preparing government funding applications for businesses?"

Yes, working with a grant writing company will cost money, but the pricing and available payment options we offer our clients meet all their needs and cash-flow scenarios. In addition, engaging professional writers from Fair Grant Writing will significantly increase the chances of your application being approved. Most importantly, you save time – the most valuable and scarce resource you have. You just need to set aside a couple of hours to be interviewed by us, provide us with the initial information and then to review the draft of the grant or loan application.

What is a better way to spend your time after a long workday – in the office putting a grant or loan application together or with your family and friends? The choice is yours.

If, after reading this book, you have any questions or need help with your application for funding, selected documents, or reports, or you just want somebody to look at your application, feel free to reach out to the author's team at www.FGWinc.ca or contact the author at igor@fgwinc.ca or call (647) 800-5006. We'll be happy to help you out.

CHAPTER 14.

SCIENTIFIC RESEARCH & EXPERIMENTAL DEVELOPMENT (SR&ED) TAX CREDIT

Definition

The Scientific Research and Experimental Development (SR&ED) Program is a federal tax incentive program designed to encourage Canadian businesses of all sizes and in all sectors to conduct research and development (R&D) in Canada.

The benefits of the Scientific Research and Experimental Development (SR&ED) tax incentive program are twofold. First, it lets you deduct SR&ED expenditures from your income for tax purposes. Second, it provides you with an SR&ED investment tax credit (ITC) that you can use to reduce your income tax payable, if any. In some cases, the remaining ITC can be refunded.

Where to Find the Funders?

Canada Revenue Agency (CRA) is the only entity in Canada authorized to process SR&ED claims.

How to Qualify for the Funding?

Even though businesses of all sizes and industries across Canada are eligible for SR&ED tax credit, the most lucrative terms are for Canadian-Controlled Private Corporation. First of all, make sure that your corporation meets the following criteria:

- it is a private corporation;

- it is a corporation that is resident in Canada and was either incorporated in Canada or resident in Canada from June 18, 1971, to the end of the tax year;
- it is not controlled directly or indirectly by one or more non-resident persons;
- it is not controlled directly or indirectly by one or more public corporations (other than a prescribed venture capital corporation);
- it is not controlled by a Canadian resident corporation that lists its shares on a designated stock exchange outside of Canada;
- it is not controlled directly or indirectly by any combination of persons described in the three preceding conditions;
- if all of its shares are owned by a non-resident person, by a public corporation (other than a prescribed venture capital corporation), or by a corporation with a class of shares listed on a designated stock exchange, were owned by one person, that person would not own sufficient shares to control the corporation; and
- no class of its shares of capital stock is listed on a designated stock exchange.

A Canadian-Controlled private corporation (CCPC) can earn a refundable ITC at the enhanced rate of 35% on qualified SR&ED expenditures, up to a maximum threshold of $3 million. A CCPC can also earn a non-refundable ITC at the basic rate of 15% on an amount over the $3 million threshold.

Other corporations can earn a non-refundable ITC at the basic rate of 15% on qualified SR&ED expenditures. The ITC can be applied to reduce tax payable.

Individuals (proprietorships) and trusts can earn a refundable ITC at the basic rate of 15% on qualified SR&ED expenditures. The ITC must be applied against tax payable and the remaining ITC can be refunded, up to a maximum of 40%.

Secondly, the research & development work you claim must meet the following definition of scientific research and experimental development (SR&ED):

"Scientific research and experimental development" means systematic investigation or research that is carried out in a field of science or technology by means of experiment or analysis and that is:

(a) basic research, namely work undertaken for the advancement of scientific knowledge without a specific practical application in view;

(b) applied research, namely work undertaken for the advancement of scientific knowledge with a specific practical application in view; or

(c) experimental development, namely, work undertaken for the purpose of achieving technological advancement for the purpose of creating new, or improving existing, materials, devices, products or processes, including incremental improvements thereto;

and, applying this definition in respect to a taxpayer, includes:

(d) work undertaken by or on behalf of the taxpayer with respect to engineering, design, operations research, mathematical analysis, computer programming, data collection, testing or psychological research, where the work is commensurate with the needs of, and directly in support of, work described in paragraph (a), (b) or (c) that is undertaken in Canada by or on behalf of the taxpayer;

but does not include work with respect to:

(e) market research or sales promotion;

(f) quality control or routine testing of materials, devices, products or processes;

(g) research in the social sciences or the humanities;

(h) prospecting, exploring, producing or drilling for minerals, petroleum or natural gas;

(i) commercial production of a new or improved material, device or product, or the commercial use of a new or improved process;

(j) style changes; or

(k) routine data collection.

What is the Funding For?

The funding is available to support research & development work that meets the definition. The following costs are eligible:

- Salary or wages of employees (including owners that draw the salary) who worked on eligible SR&ED project
- Cost of materials for SR&ED project
- Contract expenditures for basic research, applied research, experimental development or support work done on behalf of a claimant by eligible third parties
- SR&ED overhead and other direct expenditures

How to Apply?

To make an SR&ED claim, you must file an income tax return along with the following prescribed form:

Form T661, Scientific Research and Experimental Development (SR&ED) Expenditures Claim, and one of the following forms:

- Form T2SCH31, Investment Tax Credit – Corporations
- Form T2038(IND), Investment Tax Credit (Individuals)

To apply for SR&ED tax incentives, you must file the applicable prescribed forms with your income tax return by your SR&ED reporting deadline. For corporations, the reporting deadline is 18 months from the end of the tax year in which you incurred the expenditures. Individuals have 17.5 months.

Most Common Issues

The most common and most dangerous issue is the lack of proper records of research & development process and documents supporting eligible costs. This issue is usually revealed during a CRA audit, which does not always happen, but you must not take chances. Prepare your SR&ED claim assuming that there will be an audit.

In fact, CRA doesn't have a comprehensive list of the required documents. Examples of technical and financial supporting evidence are:

- Project planning documents
- Documents on design of experiments
- Experimentation plan
- Design documents and technical drawings
- Project records, laboratory notebooks
- Design, system architecture and source code (software development)
- Records of trial runs
- Project progress reports
- Minutes of project meetings
- Test protocols, data, results, analysis and conclusions
- Final project report or professional publication
- Photographs, videos
- Prototypes, samples
- Scrap, scrap records
- Contracts, lease agreements
- Records of resources allocated to the project, time sheets, activity records, payroll records
- Purchase invoices and proof of payment
- Accounting records

Even if you have everything in writing, it may not be enough to support your claim. It leaves the room for maneuvering for both the applicant and the CRA.

Small businesses do not always have the capability to properly track and record working hours, especially when the employee works on several projects at the same time. The quality, consistency and availability of the documented evidence of research & development process is another common issue.

Tips for Success

Read eligibility criteria carefully. The projects you claim must meet the criteria and the definition of research & development. The tip for success is to rate your projects based on the criteria. If you have projects that meet less than 50% of the criteria, do not claim the tax credit for those projects. Project eligibility should be determined at the start of the project as per SR&ED requirements with hypothesis and due diligence work prior to the start of a SR&ED project.

Be proactive with SR&ED tax credit. Prepare in advance and record the activities and costs of your research & development. File the records in a separate binder – in case of an audit, you can easily locate the documents you need. Do not wait until the fiscal year-end; you won't be able to remember what happened 300 days ago. Record your activities and costs as you experience them, and write the project's technical summaries on a quarterly or, even better, a monthly basis. Because recordkeeping takes so much effort, every business that considers applying for the tax credit must assess whether it's worth time to do the recordkeeping throughout the year.

Use the following tips if your business gets audited:

- If you have the records of research & development activities and their costs, you should not expect a problem. If you don't have these, the CRA will make a decision based in its auditors' assessment and the results of the audit process (including interviews with employees whose labour has been claimed).
- If you choose to use a consultant to write your SR&ED claim, make sure that you choose one who also prepares your business for the audit, and who will attend the audit

and speak with CRA directly on your behalf. This way, the consultant will address CRA's questions during audit better than you.

- Make sure that the leaders of the research & development project you claim are present at the audit. The accountants are rarely required, but you should have the person in charge of tracking labour hours, such as your human resources manager.

If you disagree with the amount of approved SR&ED tax credit claim, or the results of the audit, you have the right to appeal. You have 90 days from the date of the notice of assessment, or reassessment, to file the objection.

1. File an objection and request a secondary review or a review by a CRA group supervisor through the Appeals Branch of the CRA. CRA auditors work in groups by industry (e.g. chemicals, plastics, etc.), and each group has a supervisor.
2. File a legal claim against CRA in Canadian Tax Court. This, of course, may take months and years, not to mention the high costs. So, you need to assess whether the amount of the claim is worth the time and money that would be spent on the lawsuit.

CHAPTER 15.

CUSTOMS DUTIES DRAWBACK AND RELIEF PROGRAMS

Definition

The Duties Relief Program relieves you from having to pay duties on imported goods if you will eventually re-export the goods, either in the same condition or after using, consuming or expending them to process other goods.

The Drawback Program has the same advantages as the Duties Relief Program. The only difference is that the Drawback Program is for people who have already paid the duties and are asking for a drawback (refund) of those duties as authorized under the Customs Tariff.

Where to Find the Funders?

Canadian Border Services Agency (CBSA) is the only entity in Canada authorized to process customs duty relief and drawback applications. A customs broker licensed by CBSA can help the applicant to determine eligibility. The list of the licensed customs brokers is available at the CBSA website.

How to Qualify for the Funding?

Any Canadian entity that imports goods and pays duty is eligible, provided that:

- The applicant imports goods that are later exported as-is;
- The applicant imports goods to produce other goods for export; or

- The applicant destroys the imported goods that are obsolete or surplus, or that are manufactured into an item that is obsolete or surplus.

Note: If goods are exported to the United States or Mexico, there may be restrictions under the North American Free Trade Agreement (NAFTA). Not all goods exported to a NAFTA country are affected by limitations on drawback and duties relief. Contact a licensed customs broker to check eligibility.

The applicant must export or destroy the goods before one can file a claim.

What is the Funding For?

The funding is provided by the drawback program only. The purpose of the funding is to refund the customs duty paid by an importer that meets the eligibility criteria.

How to Apply?

To apply for the duty drawback program, fill out Form K32, Drawback Claim, and submit the form to the nearby CBSA office.

To apply for the duty relief program, fill out Form K90, Duties Relief Application, and submit the form to the nearby CBSA office.

Most Common Issues

The CBSA does not automatically refund or relieve the customs duty if the eligibility criteria are met. The applicant must take action and submit the application form. Thus, it is the applicant's responsibility to keep records of all import and export transactions, such as import and export declaration forms, and the bills of materials. The applicant may present a claim within four years (five years for destroyed goods) from the time the goods arrive in Canada.

Tips for Success

The proper recordkeeping of all export and import transactions and bills of materials (in cases where the imported product has been modified to make the exported one) is a critical success factor. Also, it is recommended to deal with a reputable, licensed customs broker for the customs clearance, duty relief applications and duty drawback claims.

CHAPTER 16.

CANADA SMALL BUSINESS FINANCING LOAN

Definition

Canada Small Business Financing (CSBF) loan is a federal government guaranteed loan that provides the financing to get a business started or help an existing business grow. The Canada Small Business Financing Loan can provide a Canadian business with up to $1,000,000 in financing for the purchase of land or business premises ($350,000 for leasehold improvements and equipment).

With assistance from the federal government, businesses can support their financing requirements without using personal assets as security.

Where to Find the Funders?

Banks, credit unions, caisses populaires and other financial institutions are eligible to make loans under the CSBF Program. In order to obtain a loan, a borrower must present his or her business proposal directly to a financial institution of his or her choice. Financial institutions are solely responsible for making the decision to approve a loan. If the loan is approved, the money the borrower receives is that of the financial institution and not the government.

How to Qualify for the Funding?

Current fiscal year gross revenues of the applicant must not exceed $10,000,000. The applicant may be a start-up or an existing business.

If the loan is for the purchase of premises, 50% of the floor space must be for the business activity.

Applications must be submitted with a business plan that includes financial statements or projections.

Eligible purchases made within the past six months can be financed.

Loan terms are generally 7-10 years depending on the asset being financed.

Maximum interest rate on variable rate loans is Prime + 3.0%; fixed rate loans is Residential Mortgage Rate + 3.0%, which includes an annual administration fee equal to an annual rate of 1.25%, which is payable to the government.

A one-time up-front government registration fee of 2% of the loan amount is payable to the government and can be added to the loan principal.

Farming businesses are not eligible under this program. However, The Canadian Agricultural Loans Act program, administered by Agriculture and Agri-Food Canada, is designed to increase the availability of loans for the purpose of farming.

What is the Funding For?

The CSBF Loan is designed to help businesses purchase, install, renovate and modernize business equipment and other fixed assets:

- Purchase or improvement of land or buildings used for commercial purposes
- Purchase or improvement of new or used equipment
- Purchase of new or existing leasehold improvements (i.e. renovations to a leased property by a tenant)
- Registration fee

You cannot use a loan to finance items like goodwill, working capital, inventories, franchise fees or assets that a holding company acquires.

How to Apply?

This program is delivered by financial institutions in partnership with the federal government. Financial institutions are required to apply the same care and procedures in making a CSBF loan as they would for conventional loans of similar amounts. An application form and a business plan or proposal are required to apply.

Most Common Issues

Decisions to lend are based on lending criteria for each financial institution. If the CSBF loan application is rejected, the applicant could contact another financial institution since lenders have different criteria related to the approval of business loans and different risk tolerances. The government does not interfere in the loan approval process.

Tips for Success

A solid and realistic business plan or proposal with the projected revenue, expenses and cash flow is required. Evidence of the growing demand for the applicant's product, and third-party endorsements of the applicant will be helpful, too.

CHAPTER 17.

GOVERNMENT FUNDING FOR NON-PROFIT ORGANIZATIONS

INTRODUCTION

Grant writing covers a wide range of fundraising activities, and continues to evolve each year. Over the last decade, paper-based submissions have been replaced with online applications, and peer-to-peer or crowd-sourced fundraising has replaced more traditional campaigns and events, but the core principals of building your request, positioning your cause and asking for funds remains the same.

The goal of this chapter is to provide non-profits with a basic understanding of the grant writing and giving process, and to provide a list of basic tools that every non-profit will need to start raising funds for their cause.

1. TOP 5 TIPS FOR FUNDRAISING

1. **Register your charity!**

   If you're still deciding if you should register your charity, the answer is "YES." Without charitable status, you will not be able to apply for municipal and provincial government grants; you cannot issue tax receipts; and you won't qualify for most corporate sponsorship opportunities. Donors of all giving levels feel more comfortable giving to registered charities. Once you get your charitable status, make sure it's on everything you send out. Contact Canada Revenue Agency to apply for charitable status.

2. Maximize the impact of your request

Foundations and corporate sponsors are accountable for their giving dollars and need to maximize the impact of their grant giving activities. Your request should maximize their return on investment to the best of your ability. Whenever possible, find a way to break down your ask to "$ per seat," "$ per camper" or "$ per participant," and then ask yourself, "Would you make this donation if you were the donor?" Almost without fail, you'll find yourself increasing your project impact outcomes every time you try this exercise.

3. Do your homework when preparing your request

Carefully research the donor's giving history before preparing your request to ensure that your ask aligns with their mission/vision, community investment priorities and amounts that they have given in the past. Giving histories of large foundations and charities can be found on the Canada Revenue Agency's Charities and Giving Page (http://www.cra-arc.gc.ca/chrts-gvng/menu-eng.html), and government grant giving organizations are required to publicly post their grantees once their funding cycle is over. Do your homework and find out if your cause is likely to receive funding before submitting a request.

4. It's all about timing

Requests are not accepted year-round. For most corporate sponsorship requests, all requests need to be submitted between mid-September and early December of each year. Most corporate sponsors get their budgets in the fall, and have to allocate all funds before January of the following year.

Government and large foundation grants have a limited window for non-profits to submit a request – usually about a month from the call date to deadline. Typically, there is an official call for proposal once they have their budget. There may or may not be a public information session that follows this, and proposals usually have to be submitted within 3 to 4 weeks. Usually calls for proposal are made in the fall (September/October) or in the spring (March/April).

Smaller private donors typically accept requests year-round and have an ongoing intake process. Once again, do your homework and keep track of when your asks should be submitted (see Section 4 for more information about preparing your lists).

5. Don't be discouraged by rejection

No matter how great you think your cause is, there is a limited pool of donors and hundreds of organizations in your area competing for the same dollars. Even if you have registered your charity, thoroughly researched your ask and submitted your request within the giving period, there is only about 30% probability that your request will be approved. Be prepared to be repeatedly discouraged – that is the nature of the fundraising process, and the only way to be successful is to send out as many requests as you can until your fundraising goals have been met. Don't give up; keep trying!

2. BASIC FUNDRAISING TOOLS

There are a few basic fundraising tools that every non-profit should have on file at the beginning of each fundraising season. Start early and work on your template letters and requests over the summer so that you have everything in place by September.

Note: The following list of tools does not apply to government grant applications or calls for proposal, which have their own application forms, requirements for request, and specific guidelines for preparing a submission.

Build your letters of request

Begin each year's fundraising campaign by developing your basic template letters of request. Typically, you need to develop a letter for corporate requests, foundation requests and renewal requests. Don't try and group all your programs into one letter. Be specific in your ask, and create customized, dedicated letters for each program, with specific outcomes associated with your request amount. Once you have your template letters, further customize them to align with the vision and investment priorities of the donors before sending them out.

Once you're happy with your final template letters, take your fundraising list and send out as many as you can throughout the year to maximize your efforts.

Have a full proposal ready

After you have created your template letters of request for the season, the next step is to expand your letter and build a full proposal. Banks, insurance companies and corporate foundations will typically request a full proposal to be submitted along with a letter of request. Full proposals will need to include a list of Board of Directors, two-year operating budget, detailed project budget, project description, work plan and sponsorship benefits. Although the preparation of a full proposal is more onerous, funding levels for grants that require a proposal are usually larger and worth the effort.

Pitchbook/PPT Presentation

A visually impactful PowerPoint presentation is also an important tool in today's world of fundraising. This tool is specific to corporate sponsors that are used to being pitched with PPT decks, and expect a meeting to be preceded by an introduction via video or PPT presentation to set the stage for your request. Similar to your template letters of request, each year's fundraising campaign should also begin with the development of a template PPT presentation. The presentation should include your organization's mission/vision, core programs, your impact on the community, request for support and sponsorship benefits. Make sure your PPT looks as good in print as it does on your computer screen. Print our your PPT in both colour and black and white to see what your donors are seeing.

Corporate sponsorship package

This fundraising tool is used primarily to raise funds to support events, conferences, professional associations and non-program-related causes. To build your sponsorship package, begin with a detailed budget of all event activities to develop your fundraising goal and sponsorship levels. A typical sponsorship package ranges from 2 to 6 pages, and includes your organization's mission/mandate and history, an overview of the event and cause, sponsorship benefits, list of sponsorship levels and contact information. Unlike a letter of request or proposal, a sponsorship package is a marketing piece and needs to be visually impactful.

3. SOURCES OF FUNDING

A good fundraising campaign will have a diversified range of funding sources to ensure a consistent cash flow, and to mitigate the impact of changing government policies and/or economic downturns. The following table outlines a range of different funding sources and the frequency in which the grants are distributed:

Funding Sources	Funding Range	Grant Turnaround Period	Grant Frequency
Major Gifts	$50,000 to Unlimited	Long-term donor relationship	Ongoing
Government Grant Applications	$10,000 to $500,000	4 to 6 months	Specified Granting Periods
Foundations and Private Funding	$5,000 to $50,000	2 to 3 months	Ongoing
Corporate Sponsorship	$5,000 to $50,000	2 to 3 months	Fall/Winter

Funding Sources	Funding Range	Grant Turnaround Period	Grant Frequency
Peer-to-Peer Fundraising	$500 to $5,000	1 to 4 weeks	Ongoing
In-Kind Donation	Unlimited	Not applicable	Ongoing

4. CREATING YOUR FUNDRAISING LIST

Each fall, your fundraising campaign should begin with your list. Your list will include fundraising prospects to be approached, their funding range, the main point of contact, submission dates and application instructions. Once you have completed your research and finalized your list, prioritize your requests and fundraising activities by upcoming deadlines and grant size. The following are two options for building your annual list.

Fundraising databases

If you have the resources, invest in a good subscription-based fundraising database. Subscription costs range from $1,000 to $10,000 per year, but will save you hours of research, vetting and cold calling. Their benefits include a searchable online database, CRM integration and grant lifecycle management. Subscription databases are regularly updated and provide you with current donor contact information, an overview of the donor's giving history and application instructions. Take the time to research what's available, and ask to take a tour of their website before committing to a subscription. Even the most expensive database cannot be updated every day. Make sure you validate and confirm funding information sourced from subscription databases when preparing your list.

DIY fundraising lists

If you do not have the resources to subscribe to a fundraising database, you can build your own fundraising list. Start by looking at who is supporting your competitors. Prepare a list of charities and non-profits with a similar mission, vision, cause or programs, and then find out who is providing them with funding support.

Funding information can often be found on their website or annual reports. If available, download at least 4 to 5 years of annual reports to get a sense of the donor funding range and commitment to the cause. Once you get a sense of which donors are providing funding for your cause, then branch out to add other like-minded organizations to your list.

Next, take the time to research each prospect's donation policy, giving instructions, deadline and primary contact information. The best time to collect this information is over the summer when the bulk of this data can be collected by summer students or volunteers.

5. THANKING AND ACKNOWLEDGING DONORS

Thank-You letters

Finally, if you are successful at receiving a grant from a donor, make sure you thank them! Do not send out template letters. Good thank-you letters set the stage for a renewal request the next year. Tell your donor how the funds will impact your organization, what they will be used for and how the donor will be acknowledged, and provide them with a copy of their tax receipt.

The thank-you letter lets your donor know that you have received their funds and confirms the use of the funds for the year. If possible, also include any marketing materials that have been developed with their name listed as a sponsor/donor. Next year, when you send them a renewal request, reference the contents of your thank-you letter and update the donor on what has been accomplished.

Social media recognition

Thanking your donors/sponsors online through social media is an easy and powerful way to acknowledge and thank your supporters. Press releases, funding announcements, events and project outcomes can be promoted through social media and linked to your donor to increase their brand exposure to your followers or members.

Print and online brand recognition

Corporate sponsorship agreements or government grant contribution agreements often have specific instructions for how their logo and brand needs to be acknowledged in print materials and online platforms. Make sure you read the agreement and instructions carefully, and get a copy of the company's/donor's/grantor's current logo in both full colour and gray scale file format. Send a copy or a web link to your donor to ensure that they are happy with their logo placements and treatment.

Final Thoughts

There are no hard and fast rules for fundraising. The same letter of request that deeply resonates with one donor could be thrown in the trash by another prospective donor. All you can do is build your lists, do your homework, ask as many people as you can for help and persevere until you have reached your fundraising goals.

SECTION 2.

NON-GOVERNMENT FUNDING

In this section, we will go through the non-government funding options for your business or organization. All of the options covered in this section are for capital funding, except for asset-based lending, which is usually an operational funding option, but in some cases, may be used for capital funding purposes. At the end of each chapter, you will find tips from funders to help you successfully apply for funding.

We intentionally skipped basic operational funding options like credit cards, term loans and lines of credit, because we trust that most of readers are familiar with them through personal experience. They work exactly the same way for the business or organization as they do for individuals – only the interest rates vary. If you want to explore credit cards, term loans or lines of credit for your business, please talk to you banker.

CHAPTER 18.
ANGEL AND VENTURE CAPITAL FUNDING

Definition

Angel funding is private funding provided by the accredited angel investors or individuals interested in investing in innovation. Angels are individuals, and they are often members of angel organizations or associations.

Venture capital funding is, on the contrary, provided by venture funds, not individuals, that invest in businesses.

Angels usually invest in earlier stages of product, technology and company development. Not only do they look for a return on their investment, but they also frequently become advisors to the start-ups that leverage their knowledge and connections to help grow the business. Venture capital firms are more interested in a higher return on investment, and for this reason, do not usually invest in companies in early stages of development.

Both types of investors are eventually looking for an exit, i.e. selling their share to a strategic buyer or the public via initial public offer (IPO) process. The lifecycle from investment to exit is, on average, 3-7 years and is longer for medical technology companies, where the government approval process may take over a year.

Where to Find the Funders?

There are 13 angel groups in Ontario, and 33 in Canada at the time of writing. For more information, contact the National Angel Capital Organization.

To find venture capital firms in Canada, connect with the Canada Venture Capital Association.

How to Qualify for the Funding?

The applicant must be either in the early stage or growth stage of business. Ideally, they are incorporated, and developing an innovative product, process or technology.

During the early stage, the company is pre-revenue and is working on product and product to market fit. Its cash flow comes from investments. Angels usually invest during the early stage.

At the growth stage, the company is already taking at least some of its revenue from sales. Driving sales is critical for this stage. The venture capital funds usually invest during this stage, and they look to fuel growth in sales.

Preferred industry sectors for angel and venture capital funding are information, communication and entertainment technologies, healthcare (medical) technologies, advanced manufacturing, finance technology and life sciences (including pharmaceuticals).

What is the Funding For?

Angel and venture capital funding is an investment in exchange for shares. It is always a custom process, so each deal has its own size and terms.

The investor and the applicant determine the use of the funding, but usually it is used for product, technology or business development. This includes employee salaries, third-party contractors' fees (for example, testing laboratory fees), travel, marketing, sales, telecommunication costs, etc.

How to Apply?

Find out if there is an application form with the venture capital or angel groups you are targeting. If there is one, fill it out and follow up with the funder to make sure they received it.

In many cases, a one-page executive summary is all that is required to apply. Supplementary information that will be required includes the business plan and the pitch deck. For certain industries, research reports, such as a "Gartner Report," may be required.

Other requirements will be determined by the funder on a case-by-case basis during the application assessment and due diligence processes.

Most Common Issues

Even though there are some common guidelines or recommendations on how to assess an application, it is up to the individual angel or venture fund to make a decision. For this reason, only 5% to 7% of all applicants are funded. For the same reason, it takes an unpredictable amount of time for the funders to make a decision. However, Maple Leaf Angels of Toronto, Ontario, now has a special program that provides a decision within 48 hours. It is expected that other angel organizations across the country will introduce similar programs.

Tips for Success

Due to the highly personalized nature of angel and venture capital funding, the availability of reputable personal references, and references for research, technology or product proposed by the applicant, are critical.

Keep in mind that the investors will eventually want to talk to the applicant, and they usually get an impression about an applicant within 30 seconds after the pitch starts. So, practice your pitch.

The applicant must have a strong management team, good business model (i.e., understands how to produce the product, who will pay for it and how to sell it), and must be able to solve real, quantifiable problems.

In the later stages of the applicant's development, they must have a clear exit strategy – usually a potential strategic investment or initial public offering (i.e., the first time the stock of a private company is offered to the public on a stock exchange). Since the positive return on capital is a goal for the angels and venture funds, the applicant must be able to demonstrate the likelihood of a positive return during the application process.

Intellectual property (IP) is a significant asset for the investor, and the applicant that may get the IP as a result of an investment is in a better position to attract funding.

Advisory boards or boards of directors are also great assets if the applicant has them. They show the ability of the applicant to attract people outside the company to help it grow, which attracts investors, too.

Success Story

In 2013, Shopify Inc. became Canada's first Internet start-up since the dot-com crash to reach a billion-dollar valuation, thanks to one of the largest venture financings in Canadian history.

The Ottawa e-commerce software company, which enables small- and medium-sized retailers to launch and manage online stores, announced Thursday that it has raised $100 million (US) in a deal led by the venture investing arm of the Ontario Municipal Employees Retirement System (OMERS Ventures) and New York's Insight Venture Partners.

Past backers, including Boston-based Bessemer Venture Partners, also invested.

CHAPTER 19.
ASSET-BASED LENDING & FACTORING

Definition

Asset-based lending is a form of financing that resembles a bank line of credit with a few important differences. The main one is that the amount of money that a company can borrow is primarily based on the value of the assets under consideration. An asset typically includes equipment, inventory, real estate or receivables (outstanding invoices to the applicant's customers). The asset-based lending backed by the receivables is called *factoring*.

Typical assets that are easily converted into cash, such as receivables, have a higher advance rate than less liquid assets, such as inventory or equipment. In most asset-based financing situations, the lender maintains control of the collections. There are usually loan covenants with this type of financing.

Asset-based lending is often faster and more flexible than a traditional bank loan. A company with good assets may receive financing in as little as 15 to 30 days.

Another benefit of asset-based lending is that it might be the only solution for companies that might not be eligible for a traditional loan. Start-ups and companies with seasonal work or poor credit can often use asset-based lending to finance their business.

Where to Find the Funders?

Asset-based lending and factoring firms are easy to find online using your favourite search engine. You can also ask your existing financial institution for a referral.

How to Qualify for the Funding?

For various types of asset-based lending, different criteria apply. For simple receivables financing and/or purchase order financing, the business can be a start-up. For more complex deals involving different assets and larger loan amounts, the business has to have been in existence for a number of years and possess assets, such as receivables, equipment, inventory or real estate.

Various funders use different approaches, and sometimes they use risk-assessment models to evaluate the company's performance, projected earnings and sales, and the owner's personal net worth. Normally, assets need to be valued, and a formal appraisal is ordered from trusted professionals to find out the market value and/or liquidation value of the asset class.

What is the Funding For?

Asset-based lending is a smart solution for companies looking to release cash tied up in their valuable possessions. Companies use asset-based lending to purchase new equipment, get working capital, finance growth, purchase materials, finance labor costs, fund acquisitions and turnaround situations, etc.

How to Apply?

Fill out an online or paper application form obtained from the funder. Usually, the funders also require copies of the following documents:

- Articles of incorporation (or master business license for partnerships)
- Two pieces of identification for all owners
- Accounts Receivable and Accounts Payable reports
- Financial statements for the past three fiscal years, reviewed or audited, for the applicant and all affiliates, offices and subsidiaries
- Assets list

The application process starts with collecting information about the business and its owners and assessing the company's industry and market for systemic risks. Each business model is unique as unique as the business's owners and customers; for the majority of small businesses, the personality of the owner and his/her management style have a great impact on the business. After the application is received, the due diligence process starts. The due diligence approach used by all financial institutions and companies suggests that all the information the owners provide be checked for potential fraud and inconsistencies. Credit and criminal record checks for the owners will likely be performed.

Most Common Issues

A normal procedure would be to request and subsequently check the company's financial statements for three consecutive years, including all affiliates, offices and subsidiaries of the corporation; obtain personal identification documents for all owners and directors; get personal net worth statements of those individuals; get all licenses, permits and registrations necessary for the particular business type; receive asset lists and values of all assets under consideration; get accounts receivable and accounts payable aging reports; approve the company's customers for the limits requested; get proof of the company's good standing with the tax authorities and other institutions responsible for the business's licensing and reporting; pay field visits to the business's facilities to make sure that the assets are truly physically present; receive independent market advice (if needed) on the value of the assets in question; inspect the premises for compliance with industry standards; confirm validity of licenses and/or permits; check court records and PPSA filings for liens; validate equipment identification numbers; contact the buyers to check and confirm purchase orders; contact the suppliers for the order placements and sale terms; receive invoices and proof of delivery and confirm those; calculate risk rating based on financial ratios and formulas, etc.

Once the due diligence process is done, the funding process is realized, based on the findings. In most cases, the funding process follows the formal Term Sheet issued at the beginning of the process and the Agreement signed by the client and the financial institution. However, there are numerous cases when, as the result of the due diligence process and following the appraisal process, the initial amounts requested are reduced to reflect the actual difference. Additionally, some conditions may be applied to request the client to execute correctional actions to free and/or change the ownership of the asset to be financed.

Tips for Success

The success of the application for funding depends on full disclosure by the business seeking financing of its material situation and their providing all the requested documents in a timely fashion.

Unfortunately, most small business owners do not volunteer information on their business and their personal situation and tend to provide it only when asked and/or when the information becomes available to the financial institution as a result of the due diligence. In this case, the accidental disclosure of any negative information tends to negatively impact the application and may lead to the complete rejection by the funder of the said application.

The best practice for the owners is to be open and honest about the business and to provide complete disclosure, including all possible challenges, problems and drawbacks. Small business owners need to see the financial institution as their partner, and need to know that any negative information will become public, and will therefore affect the application process, On the contrary, if the business owners voluntarily disclose information in anticipation of it becoming known to the lender, that will positively affect the application process.

Success Story

This success story is publicly available. However, all names have been removed.

The applicant for asset-based lending has been a pioneer and leader in the industrial digital printing industry for personalized decoration products made with textiles, ceramic, wood, glass and metal. The company sells printing systems in a strategic partnership with a $20 billion multinational imaging and electronics company.

The applicant manufactures specialized ink cartridges and private label printers co-developed with the strategic partner. These print systems serve the needs of nearly any size of business, from home-based businesses with desktop capabilities to retail and factory-scale production. Headquartered in the US, the applicant supplies an extensive global dealer network that services more than 100 countries throughout North and South America, Europe, Africa, Australia and Asia.

The applicant restructured its partnership with the strategic partner in 2016, which led to the need for a new lender that could provide a comprehensive financing solution for its global distribution requirement. Additionally, the company sought to leverage their cross-border accounts receivable, which were rapidly growing due to the success of their international expansion. The existing debt facility was constraining growth and required the company to move quickly to find a new financial partner.

Working within a tight deadline to ensure the applicant's incumbent bank was seamlessly paid off, the lender devised a plan that would provide the applicant with the financing they required to fuel their growth while addressing some of the complexities stemming from existing supplier arrangements.

Within a very short period of time, the lender presented the applicant with a one-stop solution to finance both their US and UK companies, as well as their cross-border receivables. They provided the applicant with a $5 million asset-based lending facility against accounts receivable and inventory in the US and UK, affording the company more availability than they had with their previous lender, and with fewer covenants.

CHAPTER 20.

EQUIPMENT LEASING & FINANCING

Definition

An equipment lease (including but not limited to manufacturing, transportation, office and other types of equipment) is essentially a rental agreement under which the owner of the equipment, referred to as the lessor, allows the user, referred to as the lessee, to operate or otherwise make use of the equipment in exchange for periodic lease payments, which are established at inception of the contract. During the term of the agreement the title of the equipment is the name of the leasing company or financial institution. At the end of the term, however, the lessee will exercise a purchase option to buy the equipment and will take on ownership. Simply put, and because most equipment has value far beyond a limited term, equipment leasing is the rental of equipment for a specific term and payment with the ultimate goal of ownership at the end of the agreement.

Equipment Financing is a structured loan for purchasing equipment, where the borrower (in this case the user) takes on both possession and title of the equipment immediately once purchased. In this case, the borrower repays the loan to the lender in regular or bulk loan payments based on the mutually agreed-upon structure.

Where to Find the Funders?

Normally the easiest place to find leasing companies or equipment finance institutions is a referral from the seller of the asset you are looking to lease or buy; it is in their best interests to source these types of businesses for their customers. It is always best to work with a vendor who understands your industry and has a solid track record of sales and support. If they are a well-established entity they will know where to find appropriate funding sources.

Examples of such sellers include vendors of manufacturing equipment (they will be different from industry to industry), truck and transportation equipment dealers, office equipment sellers, etc.

How to Qualify for the Funding?

To qualify for an equipment lease or equipment financing, the business must be a commercial entity (i.e., either a sole proprietor, partner or corporation).

The equipment leasing or financing company looks for an ideal combination of asset value and creditworthiness of the potential lessee or borrower.

Even though, in most cases, the equipment itself is the collateral, other assets may be required to support the application for leasing or financing.

How Much Can be Leased or Borrowed?

Equipment leasing or financing could be arranged for up to 100% of the cost of the manufacturing, transportation or office equipment and could even include software costs; in reality, it could be any asset required to support a commercial entity.

In addition, equipment leasing or financing could potentially include the cost of shipping and installing of the equipment, as well as any leasehold improvement the plant or office requires for installation (e.g., building a concrete foundation).

How to Apply?

A normal credit application will consist of approximately two pages in which the applicant provides information for the operating entity and/or ownership information.

Depending on the size of the request or the commercial credit history of the entity, additional information such as financial statements or tax returns for the business or details for the net worth of the owner or majority shareholder may be required for review.

Tips for Success

Focus on what it is you do well and source equipment that will allow growth in this area. While diversification is important there are cases where equipment is leased or secured but does not get used to its fullest and most efficient capacity, and the resources invested do not return nearly as much as other equipment in the office or plant.

It is just as important to discuss the decision to lease or finance equipment prior to entering any agreement with a trusted business adviser or accountant. They will ensure the transaction is handled best from a taxation standpoint and should be assigned the responsibility for keeping the business financial statements in order, reporting regularly on profitably and cash-flows, as well as keeping lease or loan payment records.

CHAPTER 21.

REAL ESTATE FINANCING: COMMERCIAL MORTGAGES

Definition

A commercial mortgage is a type of funding available to purchase commercial real estate. Examples of real estate include buildings or land. Real estate is collateral for commercial mortgage funding. The definition of "commercial" includes industrial buildings, retail buildings, warehouses, offices, hotels, agricultural land, land for housing construction, etc.

Where to Find the Funders?

The applicant can apply for a commercial mortgage directly with a financial insitution (such as a Canadian bank), or go through a commercial mortgage broker. The broker acts on behalf of the lender and the applicant at the same time. There are "A" lenders, such as Canadian banks, and "B" lenders, such as private financing companies, who have less capital than banks and usually pool funds from various resources, such as private funders. "B" lenders are better if there are any nuances in the future deal or if the applicant does not meet the criteria of "A" lenders.

To get the contact of a qualified commercial mortgage broker or financial institution, talk to your real estate agent, the seller of the land or property you have in mind, or the seller's real estate agent. Lastly, ask you banker for referrals within and outside the bank.

How to Qualify for the Funding?

Every lender has its own criteria for borrowers, real estate and the deal itself. Usually, there is a pre-qualification procedure, such as a credit report request, followed by a more extensive due diligence process to determine the applicant's eligibility.

What is the Funding For?

Commercial real estate financing is available for those looking to acquire a piece of real estate or acquire land for construction. It is also available to those looking to refinance existing real estate.

How to Apply?

Fill out the funder's application form to get started. Usually, the funder also require copies of financial statements for the past three fiscal years, reviewed or audited. Next, a set of individual questions must be answered by the applicant for the funder to determine the eligibility of the applicant, the real estate and the deal, and to understand the applicant's business, assets and guarantees.

Most Common Issues

Lack of information required for the commercial mortgage application is the most common issue. This becomes a challenge for the funder and the applicant, causes delays in the due diligence and approval processes, and results in extra costs.

The quality of the financial statements can also be an issue. If the financial statements are unaudited, a review notice from a third-party accountant is required.

Tips for Success

Be available and accessible to the funder. The decision-makers for your business must be involved in the commercial mortgage application and due diligence processes. There must be open, transparent communication and trust between the funder and the applicant.

The financial statements must be available and must be in good order.

BONUS CHAPTER.

WHAT IS LEAN AND HOW TO IMPLEMENT IT?

Transcript of the interview with Bill Neeve, President of Cycle Time Management, recorded in July 2017.

Igor: Hello, this is Igor Chigrin, a Business Funding Expert from Fair Grant Writing, an Ontario-based grant writing company dedicated to helping businesses grow and solve their most pressing challenges by unlocking access to government funding.

Today, we'll discuss how to avoid issues, achieve operational excellence and significantly reduce cost through the adoption of a lean-thinking approach. Lean thinking helps businesses reduce waste, time and resources required to make products or perform services. There are Canadian government grants that pay for lean consulting and lean training to implement lean thinking.

Today I am excited to have Bill Neeve, the President of Cycle Time Management on this call. Bill has over 35 years of experience in lean consulting, training and implementation. Bill, tell our listeners a couple of words about yourself and your company.

Bill: Thanks very much, Igor. First of all, it is a pleasure to be here with you today and to share information that I have gained over the last 35 years with your audience. Hopefully, they can walk away with some tips today that might help them in their business.

You asked me about my business; just a quick overview. Cycle Time Management is the name of the company, and it was started in 1986, a long time ago. We were one of the early birds to attempt to understand what Toyota was doing in their manufacturing operations. We ended up observing what they've done (and it's been an evolution, of course) and working in lean enterprise education and facilitation. We are not consultants; we're educators.

We've helped companies implement lean operating practices over the last 35 years, so we feel we've got a pretty good position and understanding of what it takes to implement and change from traditional manufacturing to using lean techniques.

Igor: That's great. So then, Bill, why don't we start with a definition. How can you define lean? What is lean?

Bill: Many companies consulting and training since the '80s, have tried to interpret what lean is. Toyota is the father of lean and developed it. Lean, in the eyes of different education groups and consulting groups, can be different things, as it can be with companies that try to implement it. The problem is there is no Lean Standard that exists as there is with quality (ISO Standard).

It's made up of many subsections like Total Productive Maintenance, Quick Change, Containerization, Pull System, Error Proofing, Five S, Machine Layout and Level Scheduling, and many more elements. It can be quite overwhelming to an organization that's first looking at it and trying to figure out how to implement it in their company. But, it's all about the process. It's about taking your traditional manufacturing operation and trying to streamline the environment, and that's the factory floor and the office; the whole company.

We've always looked at lean as a holistic company opportunity and not trying to implement lean in increments.

Igor: You mentioned Toyota invented lean. Is that how lean started in the first place? How did it start? What's the story behind lean?

Bill: The story behind lean goes back before Toyota—back to the 1920s with Henry Ford. Henry Ford came up with new and exciting production methodology. The Japanese looked at that and created their own. It's taken years and years for them to evolve into all the elements that I mentioned earlier, and there are more elements.

It's an ongoing evolution of understanding the process, and one of the big variables is people: understanding people and how they relate, and how you integrate them into the system. We'll talk about that a little bit later, I believe.

Igor: What is the main approach to lean? We've heard of different names, such as lean thinking, Six Sigma. What are those and how do you differentiate those?

Bill: Because there is no lean standard in the world, as I mentioned earlier, it's up to each company that's out there training and educating people on lean to interpret the Toyota Production System. Some of them get it right, and some of them don't. There are many approaches, but we have always looked at a company going from traditional methodology to lean by looking at the whole enterprise. We did this when we started in 1986, and it was only the last ten years, since about 2007, that people started to look beyond the factory floor.

Most consulting groups, if they come in to try and help you with improvements, look at the organization and how it's structured (vertically), not how the processes run from end to end (horizontally). We started in 1986 with the horizontal approach, which was relatively new at the time. The only other company I know of that was looking at the company for improvement horizontally at the time was Motorola.

Igor: Let's focus on Toyota's approach (Toyota production system approach). What are the key principles of Toyota production system?

Bill: Well, it boils down to probably 4 or 5 different areas. One is trying to determine what value is in your process. I keep saying it's all about process, so 1 of 2 things are happening when your people are operating in the office or the factory. They're either working on nonessential activities that shouldn't be there, or they're working on essential. Today, they call that value-added and non-value-added.

The value is one thing that they must look at very hard. Another thing is value streams. What do you need to do? There are some core value streams in your business like new product introduction, what we call the Make Ship loop (which is everything from order entry cross-functional until the product goes out the door) and there's the supply chain loop in the business.

Understanding what the high-level value streams are and then breaking the company down into core value streams and sub-value streams that connect into those. By doing that, you start to understand the flow, whether it's good or bad, where the bottlenecks are, and the whole issue of scheduling.

We talk about pull scheduling when we're talking about lean. Traditional manufacturers tend to push goods through the organization, and we help companies change to pull things through the factory, as opposed to pushing them. That's an important element.

Igor: You also mentioned waste reduction and that it is one of the important elements of the Toyota production system. Can you define waste and give us examples of what waste actually is?

Bill: When we talk about waste and lean, you mentioned earlier different subjects that are on the market and people getting confused, like Six Sigma, for example. My belief is it's to take variability out of a process.

Lean is all about waste: waste of overproduction, waste of transportation, waste when a piece of equipment is sitting idle – or people are sitting idle – waste of motion (that means taking ten steps when you only need to take one if your operation were laid out differently), overprocessing, too much inventory, defects. All of those are various types of waste that are found in what we'll call traditional organizations as opposed to somebody attempting to implement lean.

Igor: How does one identify whether the operation produces waste? What are those basic tools that our listeners can implement to identify whether there is a waste or not?

Bill: The main one that you would use is the value stream. Looking at your systems horizontally and going through and doing what we call as-is mapping with the value streams and trying to identify things that you shouldn't be doing that are a waste of time, waste of effort, or that have crept into the business over time.

It's not too often that we go back and say, "Let's take a refreshing look at what we're doing today." We put a lot of things in over the years to keep us out of trouble (little patches, let's say), and very seldom does a company go back and look at the whole company and use value streams. It's interesting what you find out when you do that.

Mapping is what we call measuring the value stream: taking a snapshot of the various value streams, looking at inventory levels, looking at processes for bottlenecks, looking at cycle time. Changeover times, if you're in a company that has presses, for example. The changeover is pretty important.

I still go into factories today that have a 20-tonne press, and it takes 8 hours to do a changeover of a die. A company that is doing lean has spent time reducing changeover time, which gives them flexibility, can do it in 10 minutes – the same press, identical. So, there is quite a difference because you do changeover and you allow yourself the flexibility to shorten your runs and move more effectively.

The first-pass yield is another thing: putting products through and meeting quality standards, reliability, having maintenance. I go into companies that have machinery down, breaking all the time. They don't have preventative maintenance, and they don't have predictable maintenance. There's much more. I could go on all afternoon.

Igor: Once waste is identified, which actions should one take to eliminate or reduce it?

Bill: I mentioned the as-is map that tells you what you think you're doing – are you actually doing it? Once you've identified the non-value-added activities, you want to create a future state, which is a streamlined version, where you're knocking out processes and non-value-added things and creating what you want the company to look like in the future in terms of the flow and how it operates.

Also, you want to form appropriate teams for project selection and look at resources available and project management techniques on how to handle them.

Igor: Speaking of resources, you mentioned that lean reduces time and resources required to complete the task. Can you illustrate how this process works?

Bill: If we take a section of a shop, for example, as you reduce processes – this could be pieces of the process. An example would be going from a 60-foot assembly line down to 10 feet. The 60-foot required 8 people to operate, so there could be a reduction in labour. That's not the point of lean, to reduce labour – it's to make the job easier for employees.

What you're trying to do is a natural outcome. You're going to reduce resources of all types. It can be equipment resources. You can have people working on more than 1 activity. It's all about productivity and improvement. That doesn't mean you get rid of the people that helped you get to where you are. I've always told people, "If you can get your operation effectively up and running, you can increase your revenues because you've got more capacity, more flexibility in your shop to take on more business." Instead of laying people off, I've seen many companies end up twice the size.

For example, I've got a client that went through a 3-year process and went from $7 million in revenue to $50 million. The reason is that they cut the cycle time of delivery and gained more opportunity in the marketplace.

Igor: We know that lean works in belts. There are different belts, and different colours like white, green, yellow, black, master black. Can you comment on how this works?

Bill: We all know about judo (with different belts) that was created in Japan and then came across the sea and around the world. In 1999, at Motorola, a gentleman named Michael Harry, who was part of the development of Six Sigma at Motorola, opened his own business and decided to use a belt system. He had a white belt, yellow belt, green belt, black belt and master black belt, and what they represent are different levels that a student would go through in a company to gain higher levels of learning and capability.

Each belt takes you up a notch in terms of your understanding of whatever the subject is. Some companies have it with Six Sigma (you get a certification saying that you've passed a white belt or yellow or green), and some training companies, such as ours, have certification in the belt system, which runs similarly.

The belt is really a level. I believe strongly everybody in the company should be at a green belt level. Then, they're educated, and they're ready to go on projects and participate in a meaningful way to implement lean.

Black belts: it's usually a small number, but they're responsible for selecting projects and understanding, monitoring and working with teams and leading teams.

A master black belt is like a mini-trainer from the outside. When we go in, we try and transfer our knowledge to a master black belt, and he takes over when we leave.

Igor: So that the company doesn't depend on the trainer for the whole time?

Bill: Yes. You don't want to have that kind of dependence.

Igor: Let's assume that our listeners decided to implement lean. What are the most common issues when implementing lean?

Bill: There can be a number of issues. Starting at the top, I know we talk about senior management needing to support the program. In my experience, it's way more than that. To do a successful implementation and transfer of operating methods, we need a senior management that can teach lean and quality. They need to lead, and the way they lead is by using some of the new tools that are out there that Toyota uses, such as Hoshin Planning: taking your strategy and integrating it with your Hoshin Planning and Deployment.

By doing that, and doing it properly, the senior management now has a role to drive what needs to be changed in the business and pass that down level by level. They need to communicate and have a total communication system embedded in the company.

Now, you asked about concerns. The people side is your biggest variability. Obviously, you want people to participate, but if you don't have leadership at the top, the people will do whatever they want.

I think inherently people want to improve their business, but they're nervous. If you have a management team and you go in a company, and they've never worked with a team concept, people are going to be afraid to participate in anything new. People always think, "Well, this is another case when the President got off an airplane, read a book and it's the project of the month." You've got to get past all of that.

One of the ways you can get past that is with a good level of education. For my life, I don't understand how a President can come back, get off a plane, tell somebody we want to do lean and not give the people on the job the tools or the knowledge.

Remember, they might have been working there 20 years, using the traditional methodology, and they don't know the difference between a streamlined process and what they're currently doing. So, you end up digging the same hole deeper and expecting better results without the proper training.

Communication can be a problem if you're not set up properly. Not managing the projects that are going to improve the business. Not allowing the resources to participate. Because you're talking about the whole company changing, you've really got to be structured for the change to make it happen.

Igor: What does lean education or lean training actually look like?

Bill: There are companies, like Hewlett Packard, that spend probably 10% of their revenue on training of all sorts, not just lean, but there are other companies that don't have budgets. They don't even have a budget for training. You can't expect people to change without opening their minds and getting new information in there.

So, lean education really plays a part, and I think I described that back in the belt system. It's a major part of the evolution of implementing lean in your company.

Igor: Okay, going back a little bit to the employee side and employee training. How do you address employee resistance to training? How do you motivate employees to apply lean thinking after training is completed?

Bill: I think one of the things you've got to do is create competition, a competitive environment. I've seen teams put together, and once they're educated on how to be a team, they can get pretty competitive, especially if the ideas on improvement come from them. They can get excited about it, and you can motivate the employees through their own participation if you know how to stickhandle through that.

Igor: We've looked at many examples in the manufacturing environment, but is lean only for the manufacturing sector, or does it work, for example, for service companies or technology companies?

Bill: That's a good question. In the beginning, when I started the company, it was hard enough to get manufacturers interested because, "It won't work here in America, or in Canada," and that sort of thing.

We've learned over the years that the principles of lean – being process oriented – work in any industry, any office, any type of business. We've worked in healthcare. Why? Because you're looking at the process. You're looking at how a patient goes through the building.

We work in wineries, trying to improve the efficiencies throughout the organization. We've worked in the food industry. We've worked in "Service Master, if You Have a Disaster," making the company more responsive to floods and getting the trucks out there quicker.

Insurance companies: in Canada, they're not as far ahead as in the States. In the States, they have used lean techniques – there are plenty case studies and examples – but we're on the verge of insurance companies opening up in a big way to the whole lean experience.

Igor: Thank you, Bill, very much. It was a great and very informative interview.

That was Bill Neeve from Cycle Time Management, interviewed by Igor Chigrin, a business funding expert with Fair Grant Writing.

RESOURCES
THE AUTHOR RECOMMENDS

LEAN BELT Certification

*Training is critical
for successful lean
performance*

LEAN BELT LEVELS

Lean Master Black Belt – Provides qualified black belt employees with the expertise to train white, yellow, green and black belts

Lean Black Belt – Provides qualified green belt employees with the expertise required to transform organizations to "Best-of-Class"

Lean Green Belt – Provides all yellow belt employees with a complete understanding of the theory and effective application of Lean concepts, principles and tools with a focus on waste

Lean Yellow Belt – Provides all white belt employees with an overview of management planning system

Lean White Belt – Provides all employees with an initial introduction and benefits of Lean

"What steps can you take to reduce customer lead time and improve quality?"

"In what ways can you improve productivity by aligning your processes and streamlining workflow to meet customer demand?

"How can you institute processes to enhance employee teamwork?"

Organizations that are applying Lean Thinking to achieve the greatest improvements in speed, efficiency and profitability share a common characteristic. Each one fully utilizes the knowledge, skills and enthusiasm of people at all levels.

Although it can be difficult to foster a common understanding of your change initiatives, it is a critical step for realizing both performance excellence and long-term bottom line results.

To effect the necessary cultural changes, organizations must commit to identifying Lean Leaders and building empowered work teams. Reaching these goals requires comprehensive training.

CTM recognizes the essential role of lean training in developing a Lean Thinking organization through our Lean Belt Program.

Yet, not all training is created equal.

The Lean Belt Certification program provides a benchmark for lean training and a common roadmap for employee development and continuous improvement. This provides a traceable standardized way to obtain lean knowledge and test an individual's understanding of lean principles.

CTM

Lean Framework

Recognition of Learning
In completion of

Lean Master Black Belt Training
to

Individual's Name

The Lean Framework Lean Belt Training   Date

Your employees will receive lean training through a blended approach of classroom and on-the-job *"Lean Learning Line"* training within your own organization, known as Train-Then-Do.

Participants will receive a *Recognition of Learning Credential* issued by Cycle Time Management Inc. upon successful completion of each level of the Lean Belt Training.

Company Industry Leader

Cycle Time Management Inc. (CTM) was co-founded by William Neeve in 1986.

Initially, CTM was primarily an educational organization doing a great deal of "missionary" work in the field of (Just In Time Manufacturing) now called Lean Enterprise a powerful, productivity improvement concept that, in 1986, was ahead of its time.

Today, CTM is a mid-sized firm, with our head office located in Kitchener, Ontario. Our clients include both American and Canadian companies, large and small, in a wide variety of business sectors.

CTM has developed a comprehensive process (The Lean Framework) that allows an organization, on a step-by-step basis, to create an environment and a means for change. Change that produces significant results in productivity improvement, employee empowerment and continuous quality improvement. Change that permeates the entire company and becomes a new paradigm for growth.

One of the training modules of the Lean Framework is the Lean Belt Certification. This is a powerful structure that is based on train then do lead by a seasoned CTM facilitator delivered onsite at client's facility

For more information
Contact William Neeve
226-747-7475
billneeve@leancycletime.com

Help Your Local Business Become Global!

Products for exporters & importers	**Coaching Sessions** for international traders	**Workshops** on export & import	**Export & Import Consulting** for businesses

Where Can You Find Reliable Buyers or Suppliers for Your Export or Import Business?

Bilateral Chambers of Commerce. In Canada, we are very fortunate to have trade associations and chambers of commerce that represent both Canada and foreign markets. The examples include Canada-EU Chamber of Commerce, Canada-India Chamber of Commerce, Canada-China Business Council, etc.

Industry association in a foreign market. For example, if you source food products from South Africa, contact SA Food Industry Association. Are you looking for the chemical industry buyers in China? Connect with China Petroleum and Chemical Industry Federation and so on.

Your existing suppliers and/or buyers. People in the industry know each other and talk to each other. So, if you are looking for the suppliers or buyers of the non-competitive product, ask your current buyers or suppliers for contacts. They can help you find new leads.

Trade or Export Promotion Agency of the country of origin or destination. Most major economies have trade or export promotion agencies. For example, Canadians, looking to export their products, can contact the Canadian Trade Commissioner Service for the contacts of the buyers abroad. Canadians, looking to import the products from Australia, can contact Austrade to get the contacts of the Australian suppliers.

Trade Directories. These are large databases of business contacts by industry, location and other metrics. They provide access to the contacts for a fee. The examples include Dun & Bradstreet, Scott's Directories, etc. You should know that the accuracy of data may sometimes be an issue, and they don't provide the background of the contact.

Internet. You can also use LinkedIn, XING, and other sources including online directories and boards. You should use them as your last option.

Any questions about Export & Import?

Ask us now at ask@winglobal.ca or call +1.647.800.7233

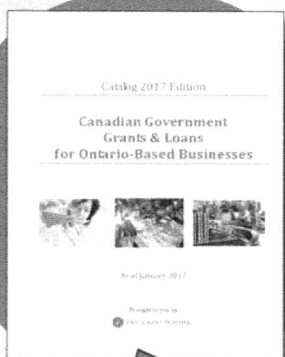

www.ingramcontent.com/pod-product-compliance
Lightning Source LLC
Chambersburg PA
CBHW021604210326
41599CB00010B/591